My United States

New York

CODY CRANE

Children's Press®
An Imprint of Scholastic Inc.

Content Consultant
James Wolfinger, PhD, Associate Dean and Professor
College of Education, DePaul University, Chicago, Illinois

Library of Congress Cataloging-in-Publication Data
Names: Crane, Cody, author.
Title: New York / by Cody Crane.
Description: New York, NY : Children's Press, an imprint of Scholastic Inc., 2018. | "A True Book." | Includes bibliographical
   references and index.
Identifiers: LCCN 2017000114 | ISBN 9780531252628 (library binding : alk. paper) | ISBN 9780531232927 (pbk. : alk. paper)
Subjects: LCSH: New York (State)—Juvenile literature.
Classification: LCC F119.3 .C73 2018 | DDC 974.7—dc23
LC record available at https://lccn.loc.gov/2017000114

Photographs ©: cover: Sylvain Sonnet/Getty Images; back cover ribbon: AliceLiddelle/Getty Images; back cover bottom: Alan Schein/Getty Images; 3 bottom: Radharc Images/Alamy Images; 3 map: Jim McMahon; 4 left: Musat/iStockphoto; 4 right: Windujedi/Dreamstime; 5 bottom: SteveByland/iStockphoto; 5 top: ClickAlps/AWL Images; 6 bottom: Education Images/Getty Images; 7 bottom: TraceRouda/Thinkstock; 7 top: Patti McConville/Alamy Images; 7 center: Nora Scarlett/Superstock, Inc.; 8-9: James Leynse/Getty Images; 11: Dosfotos/Design Pics/Getty Images; 12: Ben Girardi/Getty Images; 13: John Normile/Getty Images; 14: Michele Falzone/AWL Images; 15: Yva Momatiuk and John Eastcott/Minden Pictures; 16-17: Sean Pavone/Dreamstime; 19: Hans Pennink/AP Images; 20: Tigatelu/Dreamstime; 22: Booka1/Thinkstock; 23 top left: Steve Wisbauer/Getty Images; 23 bottom right: anna1311/Thinkstock; 23 bottom left: Windujedi/Dreamstime; 23 top right: SteveByland/iStockphoto; 23 top center: Kerrick/Getty Images; 23 center: Musat/iStockphoto; 24-25: Sarin Images/The Granger Collection; 27: Stock Montage/Getty Images; 29: Henry Hudson (1570-1611) (gouache on paper), Baraldi, Severino (b.1930)/Private Collection/ © Look and Learn/Bridgeman Art Library; 30: Sarin Images/The Granger Collection; 31 left: Booka1/Thinkstock; 31 right: Mary Altaffer/AP Images; 32: Mary Altaffer/AP Images; 33: PhotoQuest/Getty Images; 34-35: Theo Wargo/Getty Images; 36: Rolf52/Dreamstime; 37: ClickAlps/AWL Images; 38: The Washington Post/Getty Images; 39: Ramin Talaie/Getty Images; 40 bottom: Hortimages/Shutterstock; 40 background: PepitoPhotos/iStockphoto; 41: Tomas Abad/age fotostock; 42 top left: Library of Congress; 42 top right: Library of Congress; 42 center left: C.M. Bell (Firm : Washington, D.C.)Library of Congress; 42 center right: World History Archive/Alamy Images; 42 bottom: Bettmann/Getty Images; 43 top left: Underwood Archives/Getty Images; 43 top right: GL Archive/Alamy Images; 43 center left: Martha Holmes/Getty Images; 43 bottom left: Moviestore collection Ltd/ Alamy Images; 43 bottom center: Courtesy Nasa/Jpl-Caltech/ZUMA Press/Newscom; 43 center right: Brent N. Clarke/Getty Images; 43 bottom right: Dimitrios Kambouris/Getty Images; 44 bottom left: TammeW/Thinkstock; 44 bottom right: cocozero/ Shutterstock; 44 top: Sean Pavone/Dreamstime; 45 top: manoa/Getty Images; 45 center: Misunseo/Shutterstock; 45 bottom: James Leynse/Getty Images.

Maps by Map Hero, Inc.

Front cover: New York City skyline
Back cover: The Statue of Liberty

Welcome to New York

Find the Truth!

Everything you are about to read is true **except** for one of the sentences on this page.

Which one is **TRUE**?

T or F Most of New York is wilderness and farmland.

T or F New York is the most populated state in the country.

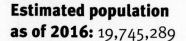

Key Facts

Capital: Albany

Estimated population as of 2016: 19,745,289

Nickname: The Empire State

Biggest cities: New York City, Buffalo, Rochester

UNITED STATES

New York

NEW YORK

FTX·9145

EMPIRE STATE

Find the answers in this book.

Contents

THE BIG TRUTH!

What Represents New York?

The beaver
is New York's
state animal.

New York's state
flower is the rose.

4

New York City's Macy's Thanksgiving Day Parade

The eastern bluebird is New York's state bird.

This Is New York!

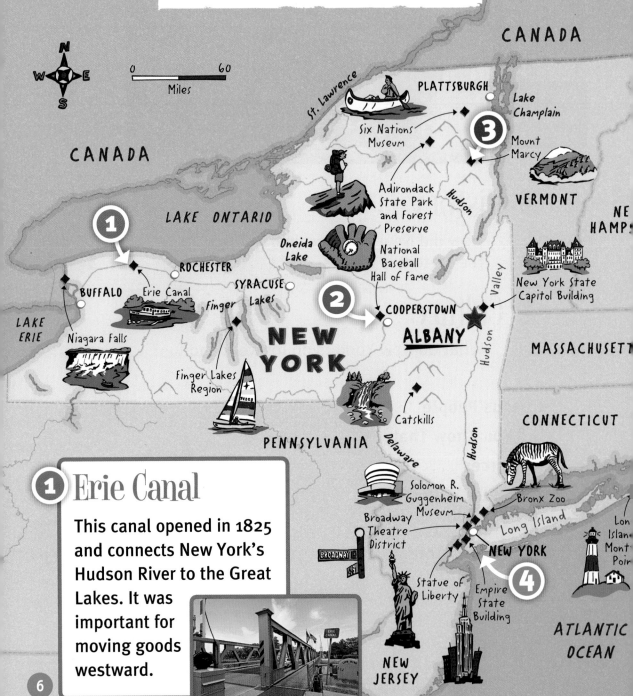

CANADA

N W E S

0 — 60
Miles

St. Lawrence

PLATTSBURGH

Lake Champlain

Six Nations Museum

3

Mount Marcy

CANADA

LAKE ONTARIO

Adirondack State Park and Forest Preserve

VERMONT

NE HAMPS

Oneida Lake

National Baseball Hall of Fame

Hudson

1

ROCHESTER

SYRACUSE

New York State Capitol Building

BUFFALO

Erie Canal

Finger Lakes

2

COOPERSTOWN

Valley

LAKE ERIE

Niagara Falls

NEW YORK

ALBANY

Hudson

MASSACHUSETT

Finger Lakes Region

Catskills

CONNECTICUT

PENNSYLVANIA

Delaware

Hudson

Bronx Zoo

Long Island

Lon Islan Mont Poir

Solomon R. Guggenheim Museum

Broadway Theatre District

NEW YORK

4

BROADWAY

Statue of Liberty

Empire State Building

ATLANTIC OCEAN

NEW JERSEY

1 Erie Canal

This canal opened in 1825 and connects New York's Hudson River to the Great Lakes. It was important for moving goods westward.

ERIE CANAL

❷ National Baseball Hall of Fame

Located in Cooperstown, this museum captures the history of America's pastime and its greatest players.

❸ Mount Marcy

This peak is New York's highest, at 5,344 feet (1,629 meters). It is part of the ancient Adirondack Mountains, which are roughly 1 billion years old.

❹ New York City

As the largest city in the United States (and one of the largest on Earth), New York City is packed full of things to do and see. There are countless museums, entertainment options, and historical landmarks.

New York City has a population of more than eight million people.

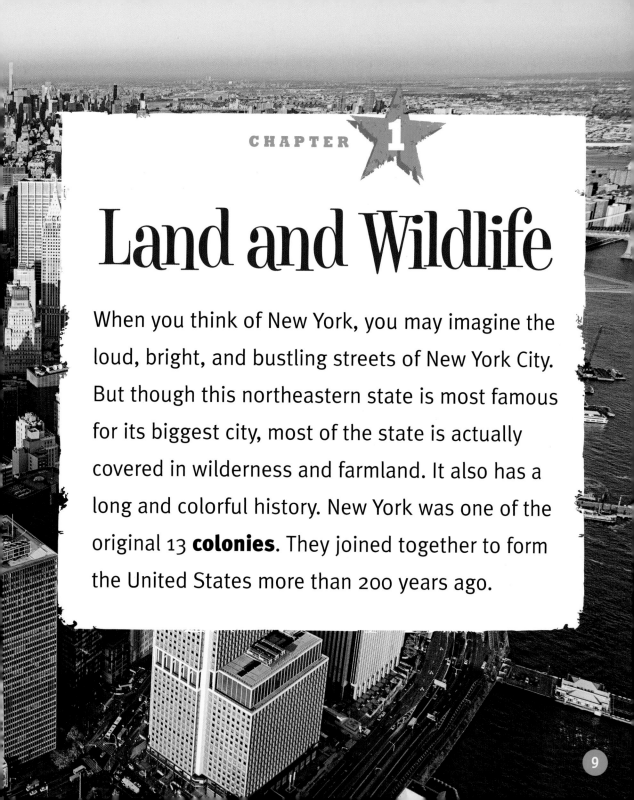

CHAPTER 1

Land and Wildlife

When you think of New York, you may imagine the loud, bright, and bustling streets of New York City. But though this northeastern state is most famous for its biggest city, most of the state is actually covered in wilderness and farmland. It also has a long and colorful history. New York was one of the original 13 **colonies**. They joined together to form the United States more than 200 years ago.

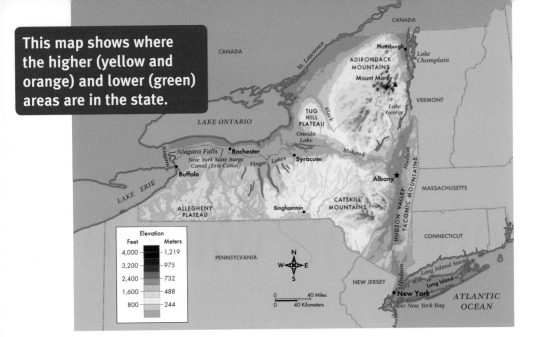

This map shows where the higher (yellow and orange) and lower (green) areas are in the state.

Stunning Landscape

New York has beautiful scenery. Two mountain ranges cross the state's interior. They are called the Catskills and the Adirondacks. Within them are deep valleys, sparkling lakes, and rushing waterfalls. Many of these features formed thousands of years ago. Back then, New York was covered in thick ice. These **glaciers** slowly grew and shrank over time. Their movement carved out lake beds, widened valleys, and rounded off mountains.

Famous Falls

One of New York's most amazing natural features is Niagara Falls. These huge waterfalls tower 175 feet (53 m) above the ground. That is about 17 stories high! Niagara is actually made up of three waterfalls. They are named the American, Bridal Veil, and Horseshoe (or Canadian) Falls. The falls span the U.S.–Canadian border on the Niagara River. The river flows from Lake Erie to Lake Ontario. About 150,000 gallons (567,812 liters) of water rush over Niagara Falls every second!

About 12 million tourists visit Niagara Falls each year.

From Lakes to Rivers

Lake Erie and Lake Ontario, two of the five Great Lakes, border New York's northwestern side. Other large lakes in the state include Lake Champlain, Lake George, Oneida Lake, and Lake Placid. Central New York also has 11 Finger Lakes, named for their finger-like shape. Millions of campers, hikers, and boaters vacation here each year. The Hudson River is New York's longest river. It stretches for 306 miles (492 kilometers) and empties into the Atlantic Ocean.

Skaneateles Lake, one of the Finger Lakes, has such clean water that local communities take drinking water straight from the lake.

Residents work to shovel away some 5 feet (1.5 m) of snow on a rooftop.

MAXIMUM TEMPERATURE
108°F

MINIMUM TEMPERATURE
-52°F

Seasonal Climate

New York experiences four distinct seasons. Spring is mild and warm, while summer is sunny and hot. Fall is crisp, leading to a cold and snowy winter. In January, the coldest month, the average temperature is 35 degrees Fahrenheit (2 degrees Celsius). The northern part of the state often sees severe snowstorms called blizzards in winter. July is the hottest month, when average temperatures reach 76°F (24°C). Overall, the state gets about 40 inches (102 centimeters) of **precipitation** each year.

13

Vast Woodlands

Forests cover more than half of New York. About 100 different kinds of trees grow in the state. Many of these trees have leaves that change color in the fall. They create a bright red, orange, and yellow display. These colors attract many visitors. Many types of **native** wildflowers, mosses, and shrubs also grow in the state. Along the coast are swampy, grass-filled wetlands.

New York's forests burst into color during the fall.

Deer sometimes wander into backyards.

Rich in Wildlife

New York's forests and waterways teem with life. Deer and moose hunt tasty greens. Coyotes eat plants as well as small creatures. Some animals even make their way into New York City! The state also sits along a busy bird **migration** route. More than 200 types of birds pass through each year. The eastern bluebird is sometimes a sign of spring. It's among the first migrating birds to return north.

When the New York State capitol was completed in 1899, it was the most expensive U.S. government building of its time.

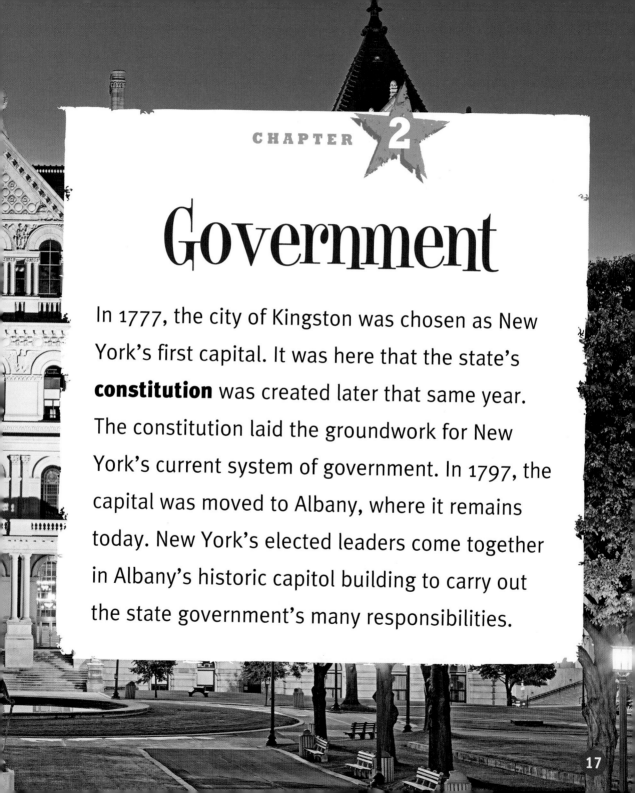

CHAPTER 2

Government

In 1777, the city of Kingston was chosen as New York's first capital. It was here that the state's **constitution** was created later that same year. The constitution laid the groundwork for New York's current system of government. In 1797, the capital was moved to Albany, where it remains today. New York's elected leaders come together in Albany's historic capitol building to carry out the state government's many responsibilities.

The Three Branches of Government

New York's government is divided into executive, legislative, and judicial branches. Each branch has different powers and responsibilities. This keeps any one of them from having too much control over the state.

Led by the governor, the executive branch carries out laws. The legislative branch, made up of a 63-member senate and a 150-member assembly, is in charge of making laws. The judicial branch interprets the state's laws in court cases.

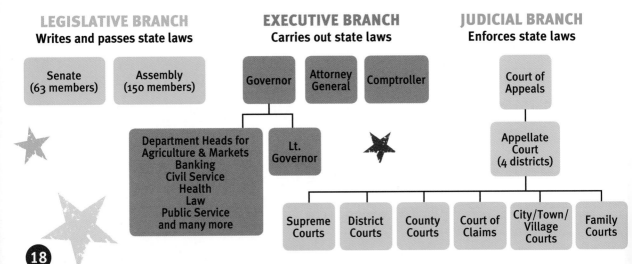

NEW YORK'S STATE GOVERNMENT

LEGISLATIVE BRANCH
Writes and passes state laws

- Senate (63 members)
- Assembly (150 members)

EXECUTIVE BRANCH
Carries out state laws

- Governor
- Attorney General
- Comptroller
- Department Heads for Agriculture & Markets, Banking, Civil Service, Health, Law, Public Service and many more
- Lt. Governor
- Supreme Courts
- District Courts
- County Courts
- Court of Claims
- City/Town/Village Courts
- Family Courts

JUDICIAL BRANCH
Enforces state laws

- Court of Appeals
- Appellate Court (4 districts)

Many legislators worked in other professions before being elected to the state assembly.

Governing a Huge Population

With more than 19 million residents, New York has the third-largest population of the U.S. states. Its annual budget is more than $130 billion, which is larger than that of many countries. This means governing New York is a major responsibility. The state's leaders must carefully consider their decisions to ensure that everyone is represented fairly, from the people of New York City to residents of the most rural areas.

New York in the National Government

Each state sends elected officials to represent it in the U.S. Congress. Like every state, New York has two senators. The U.S. House of Representatives relies on a state's population to determine its numbers. New York has 27 representatives in the House.

Every four years, states vote on the next U.S. president. Each state is granted a number of electoral votes based on its number of members in Congress. With two senators and 27 representatives, New York has 29 electoral votes.

2 senators and 27 representatives

29 electoral votes

With 29 electoral votes, New York's voice in presidential elections is above average compared to other states.

Representing New York

Elected officials in New York represent a population with a range of interests, lifestyles, and backgrounds.

Ethnicity (2015 estimates)

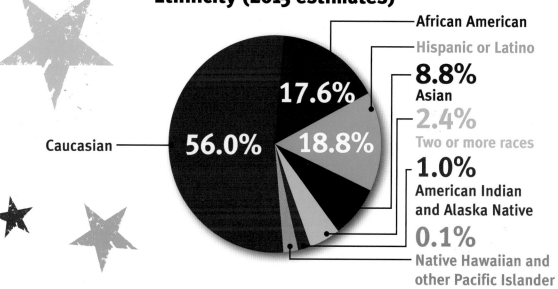

- Caucasian **56.0%**
- **17.6%** African American
- **18.8%** Hispanic or Latino
- **8.8%** Asian
- **2.4%** Two or more races
- **1.0%** American Indian and Alaska Native
- **0.1%** Native Hawaiian and other Pacific Islander

34% of the population have a degree beyond high school.

23% of New York residents were born in other countries.

54% own their own homes.

88% live in cities.

86% of the population graduated high school.

30% speak a language other than English at home.

What Represents New York?

States choose specific animals, plants, and objects to represent the values and characteristics of the land and its people. Find out why these symbols were chosen to represent New York or discover surprising curiosities about them.

Seal

The shield shows two trade ships sailing the Hudson River. Two women, Liberty and Justice, stand on either side of the shield. Liberty is stepping on a crown. This symbolizes victory over Great Britain during the Revolutionary War. Justice is blindfolded and holds a scale to symbolize fairness. Below them is New York's motto, *Excelsior*, which is Latin for "ever upward."

Flag

New York's state flag shows the state seal against a field of blue. It was adopted in 1901.

22

Milk
STATE BEVERAGE
New York is one of the country's top milk producers.

Garnet
STATE GEM
The Adirondack Mountains are home to the world's largest garnet mine.

Eastern Bluebird
STATE BIRD
In 1970, New York named the eastern bluebird its state bird. It was the last state to declare a state bird.

Rose
STATE FLOWER
The rose is also the national flower of the United States.

Beaver
STATE ANIMAL
Fur traders wiped out beavers from most of New York in the 1600s.

Apple
STATE FRUIT
One of New York City's nicknames is the Big Apple.

Native Americans living in
what is now New York traded
with early European explorers.

History

People first moved into the New York area about 5,000 years ago. By the 1500s, when European explorers first arrived, several Native American cultures had developed throughout the region. By 1783, the United States had become an independent country. New York **ratified** the U.S. Constitution in 1788. That officially made New York the new nation's 11th state.

First People

The earliest residents of what is now New York were hunter-gatherers. They caught wild game and fished. They also collected nuts, berries, and roots. These native people set up temporary villages that could be moved around as they hunted. Some people eventually began farming crops such as corn, beans, and squash. Farming allowed native people to remain in one place. Native groups traded with one another and sometimes fought over land.

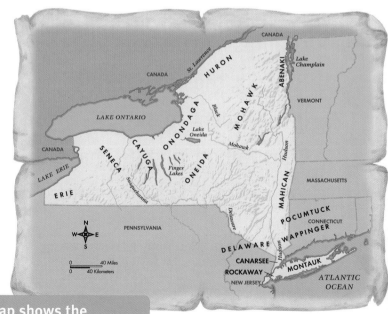

This map shows the general areas where Native American groups settled.

Several related families lived together inside a longhouse.

Iroquois Tribes

Different Native American groups moved into the New York region thousands of years later. They spoke the Iroquois language. Iroquois people lived in homes called longhouses. The people belonged to clans, or extended families, that were named after animals, such as wolf, bear, or turtle. These groups followed a mother's family line. Women raised children, cooked, and tended crops. Men hunted, fished, and protected the villages.

A Model Government

In 1570, five Iroquois groups decided to band together, forming the Iroquois League. It functioned as a **democracy**. Each group elected officials. The elected leaders of all five groups met and made decisions on how to lead their people. When the United States first formed, its Founding Fathers studied the Iroquois's political system. Some experts think the Iroquois League may have served as a model for the U.S. government. The U.S. states would join together, with each given an equal voice in the country's leadership.

This map shows the routes that European explorers took through what is now New York.

New York's Hudson River is named after European explorer Henry Hudson (in blue).

European Settlers

An explorer named Henry Hudson sailed from Europe in 1609. He reached what would become New York and claimed the land for the Netherlands. Soon after, the Dutch colony of New Netherlands was founded there. Its first city was New Amsterdam. People from many nations began making their way to the colony in search of new opportunities. These new residents came from Ireland, Denmark, Sweden, Germany, Norway, and France. Traders also brought enslaved people from Africa.

From Colony to State

New Amsterdam became a successful Dutch shipping center. This success led Great Britain to forcefully take the colony for its own in 1664. The British changed the name of the colony and its largest city to New York.

By the 1760s, colonists had begun to challenge British rule. In 1776, New York and 12 other colonies declared themselves a separate nation from Great Britain. They fought against the British in the Revolutionary War and gained independence in 1783.

Timeline of New York Events

ca. 3000 BCE
The first people arrive in New York.

1664
Great Britain takes control of New York.

ca. 3000 BCE → 1570 CE → 1609 → 1664

1570 CE
The Iroquois League is formed.

1609
Henry Hudson explores New York.

Boomtown

The New York Stock Exchange was created in 1792 in New York City. It allowed people to invest money in businesses. This attracted banks and industries to the city. **Immigrants** from across Europe came, too, hoping to escape hunger and poverty in their home countries. These people helped build the city's famous skyscrapers and bridges. The Statue of Liberty stands in New York Harbor. It welcomes those starting new lives in the United States. France presented the statue as a gift to the American people in 1886.

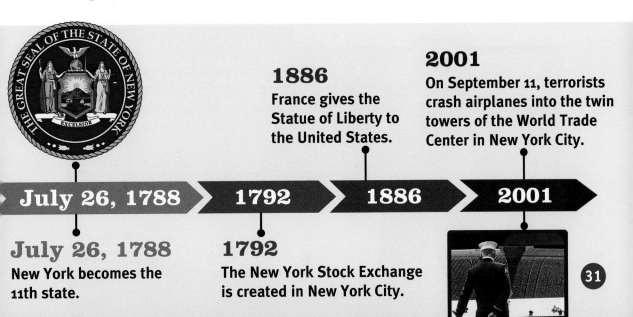

1886
France gives the Statue of Liberty to the United States.

2001
On September 11, terrorists crash airplanes into the twin towers of the World Trade Center in New York City.

July 26, 1788 1792 1886 2001

July 26, 1788
New York becomes the 11th state.

1792
The New York Stock Exchange is created in New York City.

Modern Times

New York has seen many ups and downs. A catastrophic drop in stock market prices helped trigger the Great Depression in 1929. People across the country lost their jobs and savings. On September 11, 2001, terrorists attacked New York City's World Trade Center. A memorial there honors the nearly 3,000 people who were killed. Bad investments caused some of the country's largest banks to go **bankrupt** in 2008. But New York City continues to thrive. It remains one of the world's largest financial and cultural centers.

A firefighter reads the names of firefighters who died in the September 11, 2001, attack on the World Trade Center.

Washington Irving

Washington Irving was born on April 3, 1783, in New York City. He was named after George Washington, who had been a hero of the Revolutionary War. Irving became famous after writing several short stories that were published in 1819 and 1820. They included Irving's best-known works, "Rip Van Winkle" and "The Legend of Sleepy Hollow." The stories centered on villagers living in New York during colonial times.

One-third of all actors in the United States live in New York.

CHAPTER 4

Culture

People from nearly every background live in New York. This **diversity** has helped the state grow. It has also produced some of our nation's most celebrated people. Five U.S. presidents were born in New York. Many famous musicians, from cellist Yo-Yo Ma to rapper Jay-Z, also call the state home. When it comes to theater, business, fashion, and more, New York is the place to be.

New York City native Lin-Manuel Miranda created and starred in the hit Broadway musical *Hamilton*

A Place for Sports

New York boasts three professional football teams: the New York Giants, the New York Jets, and the Buffalo Bills. Baseball fans can watch the New York Mets or the New York Yankees. For basketball, there are the New York Knicks, the Brooklyn Nets, and the New York Liberty. Three National Hockey League teams play in the state. New York has also been the home of sports legends such as baseball player Lou Gehrig.

When the Yankees began playing in New York City in 1903, they were called the Highlanders.

New York City's Macy's Thanksgiving Day Parade features giant balloons of popular characters.

New York Celebrations

Like all states, New York has plenty of local traditions. Many of New York City's annual holiday celebrations have become world famous. For example, huge numbers of people tune in on their televisions to watch the city's Thanksgiving Day Parade and the Christmas tree lighting ceremony at Rockefeller Center. Other New York traditions include festivals highlighting the state's agricultural products, the yearly ceremony admitting new members at the Baseball Hall of Fame, and more.

Fox News is one of the many media companies located in New York City.

Big Businesses

New York has the third-largest state **economy**, after California and Texas. New York City is a world center for the financial industry. Billions of dollars are exchanged on the New York Stock Exchange every day. The city is known for fashion, advertising, and media jobs, too. In addition, many news programs and television shows are filmed there. It is also the main location for publishing in the United States. Many book, magazine, and newspaper offices are located there.

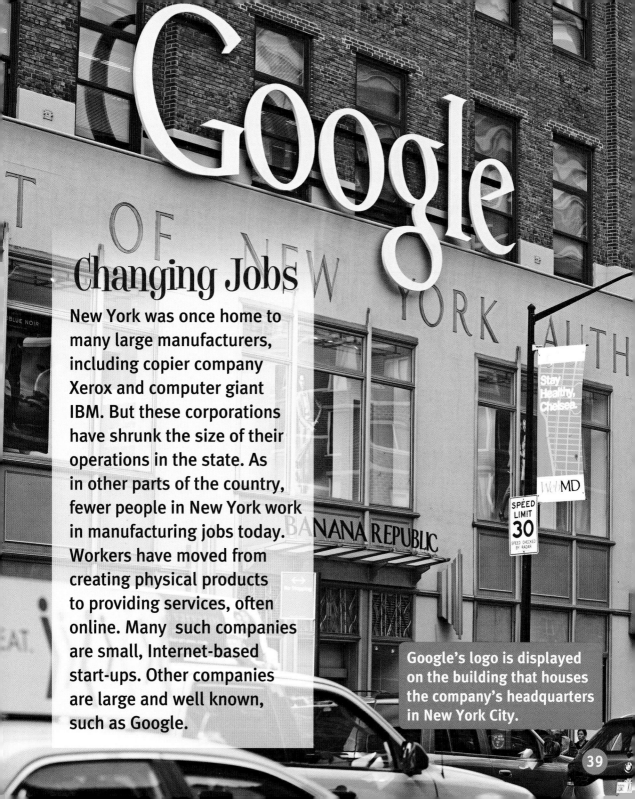

Changing Jobs

New York was once home to many large manufacturers, including copier company Xerox and computer giant IBM. But these corporations have shrunk the size of their operations in the state. As in other parts of the country, fewer people in New York work in manufacturing jobs today. Workers have moved from creating physical products to providing services, often online. Many such companies are small, Internet-based start-ups. Other companies are large and well known, such as Google.

Google's logo is displayed on the building that houses the company's headquarters in New York City.

A World of Food

New York's food reflects the many types of people who live there. Italians have made New York famous for pizza. Jewish delis serve up bagels with cream cheese, smoked salmon, and other toppings. Spicy Buffalo chicken wings are a local specialty from the city of Buffalo. New York's many farms provide fresh dairy products and produce. There is also seafood from the coast.

 Egg Cream

Despite its name, this classic New York treat doesn't have any eggs in it. It only has three ingredients, so it is easy to make at home.

Ingredients

1/2 cup milk   Seltzer water
Chocolate syrup

Directions

Mix the milk and syrup in a glass to make chocolate milk. Then add seltzer to fill the rest of the glass. Mix and enjoy! Feel free to add more syrup if you want a stronger chocolate flavor.

The Metropolitan Museum of Art in New York City holds hundreds of thousands of pieces in its collection.

Why the State Is Great

New York's economy made about $1.5 trillion in 2016. That is about as much as was made in Canada, the country with the 10th-largest economy in the world! New York is filled with creative and inspiring people. It is a place where important business decisions are made. These can impact people around the world. It is also a state filled with natural beauty and farmland. All these things are what make New York such an amazing state! ★

Famous People

Sojourner Truth

(1797?–1883) was a former slave who became an anti-slavery and women's rights activist. She was born in New York.

Walt Whitman

(1819–1892) was a poet whose best-known works include *Leaves of Grass* and "O Captain! My Captain!" He was born on Long Island.

Susan B. Anthony

(1820–1906) was a leader in the fight for women's right to vote. She grew up in Battenville.

George Gershwin

(1898–1937) was a popular composer known for *Rhapsody in Blue* and the opera *Porgy and Bess*. He was born in New York City.

Edward "Duke" Ellington

(1899–1974) was a jazz bandleader and composer. He lived in New York City for much of his life.

Langston Hughes

(1902–1967) was a poet who gained recognition during the Harlem Renaissance of the 1920s.

Jackson Pollack

(1912–1956) was a painter in the abstract expressionist movement. He lived in New York for many years.

Robert Oppenheimer

(1904–1967) was a physicist at the University of California who led the World War II project that developed the first atomic bomb. He was born In New York City.

Mel Brooks

(1926–) is a comedian and award-winning film director and producer. He was born and raised in New York City.

Carl Sagan

(1934–1996) was an astronomer and author. He is best known for the TV series *Cosmos: A Personal Voyage*. He was born in New York City.

Spike Lee

(1957–) is a film director, actor, writer, and producer who is famous for films such as *Do the Right Thing* and *Malcolm X*. He has lived in New York City since he was a child.

Mariah Carey

(1970–) is a Grammy Award-winning pop and R&B singer. She was born in Huntington.

Did You Know That ..

It took 31 years to construct the state capitol in Albany.

New York City's subway system has more than 660 miles (1,062 km) of track.

At a height of 1,250 feet (381 m), the Empire State Building was the tallest building in the world when it was completed in 1931.

Niagara Falls State Park, created in 1885, is the oldest state park in the United States.

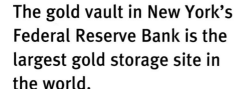

The gold vault in New York's Federal Reserve Bank is the largest gold storage site in the world.

Did you find the truth?

 Most of New York is wilderness and farmland.

New York is the most populated state in the country.

Resources

Books

Nonfiction

Cunningham, Kevin. *The New York Colony*. New York: Scholastic, 2011.

Levine, Ellen. *If You Lived With the Iroquois*. New York: Scholastic, 1999.

Somervill, Barbara A. *New York*. New York: Children's Press, 2014.

Fiction

Konigsburg, E. L. *From the Mixed-Up Files of Mrs. Basil E. Frankweiler*. New York: Atheneum, 1967.

McKissack, Patricia. *Look to the Hills: The Diary of Lozette Moreau, a French Slave Girl*. New York: Scholastic, Inc., 2004.

Movies

The Avengers (2012)

Ghostbusters (1984)

The Great Gatsby (1974)

Home Alone 2: Lost in New York (1992)

Miracle on 34th Street (1947)

Newsies (1992)

Sabrina (1954)

Spider-Man (2002)

Visit this Scholastic website for more information on New York:

★ www.factsfornow.scholastic.com
Enter the keywords **New York**

Important Words

bankrupt (BANGK-ruhpt) unable to pay back money owed to others

colonies (KAH-luh-neez) communities settled in a new land but with ties to another government

constitution (kahn-sti-TOO-shuhn) the principles under which a nation or state is governed

democracy (dih-MAH-kruh-see) a form of government where people exercise power through elected officials

diversity (dih-VUR-suh-tee) the inclusion of people from more than one nationality, ethnicity, religion, or background

economy (ih-KAH-nuh-mee) the system of buying, selling, making things, and managing money in a place

glaciers (GLAY-shurz) slow-moving masses of ice

immigrants (IM-uh-gruhntz) people who move from one country to another and settle there

migration (mye-GRAY-shuhn) a large group of people or animals moving together from one place to another

native (NAY-tiv) living or growing naturally in a region

precipitation (pri-sip-uh-TAY-shuhn) all water that falls to Earth, including rain, snow, dew, and fog

ratified (RAT-uh-fied) officially approved

Index

Page numbers in **bold** indicate illustrations.

About the Author

Cody Crane is an award-winning children's writer. She specializes in nonfiction and has written about everything from hibernating bears to roller coasters. Before becoming an author, she was set on becoming a scientist. But she discovered that sharing science, art, history, and a huge range of other topics with a young audience was even better. Crane lives in Houston, Texas, with her husband and son.